like love poems

like love poems

selected poems

JOANNA MARGARET PAUL

EDITED BY BERNADETTE HALL

VICTORIA UNIVERSITY PRESS

VICTORIA UNIVERSITY PRESS
Victoria University of Wellington
PO Box 600 Wellington
vuw.ac.nz/vup

National Library of New Zealand Cataloguing-in-Publication Data

Paul, Joanna Margaret, 1945-2003.
Like love poems : selected poems / Joanna Margaret Paul ;
edited by Bernadette Hall.
Includes index.
ISBN 13: 978-0-86473-527-0
ISBN 10: 0-86473-527-8
I. Hall, Bernadette. II. Title.
NZ821.2—dc 22

Published with the assistance of a grant by

ARTS COUNCIL OF NEW ZEALAND *TOI AOTEAROA*

Printed by Printlink, Wellington

Contents

The flowers remember
The sugar-bowl remembers

Introduction

I'm reading essays by Calvani [Calvino] do you know him
– on LIGHTNESS – QUICKNESS – EXACTITUDE
– VISIBILITY – MULTIPLICITY Meanwhile roses
crowd around but Im strangely unimpelled to paint. Will
go into the bush later to fill a rather exciting commission.
Meanwhile I have a request for you that might seem
quaint. Would you like to be my literary executor! A poet-
lawyer friend has offered to make my will! I thought of
disposing my children – then my poems feel free to refuse
if this seems too onerous or if our age clearly makes the
request absurd. Charles is the 2nd choice for youth.

There is no date on this letter, one of so many I have stored away in
the big box labelled, 'Joanna'. It still makes me laugh. Joanna and
I were almost twins, born in the same year and only days apart.
Both Sagittarians. What a practical housewife she was turning out
to be! And sadly, what a short step from opening the letter and
going into the abandoned house in Maxwell Avenue, Wanganui
with Charles Bisley as my quintessential ally.

There was already a damp smell in the air, stashes of paper
everywhere, some sheets marked already with a fine blue rash of
mould. The hall cupboards, like huge linen presses, were filled up
to the roof with papers, many neatly sorted and arranged in labelled
manila folders. There were poems on the back of envelopes, down
the margins of letters, the wedding guest-list beside the phone
was itself a poem, in Joanna's distinctive calligraphy. There were
marbled hard-covered little books to be opened up and inside, page
after fascinating page, paintings one side, poems on the other.

Most of my poetry is love poetry. Most aside from small
magazines and readings in the South Island of the seventies
unpublished. I was clear about wanting to publish my
waiata tangi for my infant daughter, Imogen (Alan Loney
did it magnificently.) Clear about wanting to put out my
lament for the poet Iain Lonie, BLUE MOURNING. But
female diffidence or Presbyterian reticence have made me
hold onto a decade of work, LIKE LOVE POEMS, so is
the germ of each embedded in its circumstance.

Such is the explanation Joanna herself provided for the absence of
her poetry from the literary scene in her essay, 'On Not Being a
Catholic Writer' (*The Source of the Song: New Zealand Writers on
Catholicism*, edited by Mark Williams, Victoria University Press,
1995, p. 136). She lists Graham Lindsay's journal *Morepork* and
Simon Garrett's *untold* as having been vehicles for her work in the
1970s. Subsequently a few poems appeared in *Parallax, Landfall,
Sport* and *Takahe*. She is also to be found in *The New Poets:
Initiatives in New Zealand Poetry* (edited by Murray Edmond
and Mary Paul, Allen & Unwin, 1987), *Yellow Pencils* (edited by
Lydia Wevers, Oxford, 1988), and the latest Penguin and Oxford
anthologies of New Zealand poetry. Sharp-eyed Patrick Evans
noted in *The Penguin History of New Zealand Literature* (1990)
that the method she used, like that of Fiona Farrell and Dinah
Hawken, 'enables linking to surroundings without bearing-down
on the subject like that of some male poets of the Seventies'.

Time and time again, Joanna tried to get one particular group of
poems out into the public arena. In a biographical note in *Landfall*
193 (1997), she wrote of 'a book still in preparation called *Like
Love Poems*, poems written from time to time over a period of 15
years'. This suggests a starting point as early as 1982, two years
before the end of her marriage.

Round about 1996 she wrote to me:

Dear Bernadette Thank you so much for coming round the
evening. We enjoyed yr presence @ dinner & I am grateful
for your refining eye on my poems once again. I am feeling
surfeited w. my own voice – & that one insistent theme! . . .

... Perhaps I feel the same about the poems they deal w such elusive subject matter that to speak is to exaggerate – I do enjoy yr company my friend & hate to feel I wear you out!

I hope I didn't sigh, not even ever so slightly, when the love poems were produced for further consideration. Many of them were riveting, and I have included them in this book. But others were not. And to be honest, that was my greatest fear when I was struck with the idea of editing a substantial book for Joanna. Would there be enough poems to get past that questionable 'refining eye' of mine?

I decided early on that in this collection Joanna's work would be presented in a conventional format, the poems to stand by themselves, as groupings of words on the page, to be read with active attention to their linguistic possibilities, their layered meanings. Poems like those in 'Unwrapping the Body' that depend on calligraphy and visual inventiveness, notes, scribbles, crossings out, etc, I would leave for others to present in alternative formats. Some have already appeared in *Brief* 32 (Winter 2005), edited by Jack Ross. Others will be available under her name at the NZEPC website <www.nzepc.auckland.ac.nz>. The beautiful little books crafted by Brendan O'Brien, and *Imogen* of course, so well-handled by Alan Loney, show what can happen when text is understood as visual art. My aim was different.

I took heart from the fact that Joanna herself had approved of a more writerly format when she entrusted poems to the journals and anthologies mentioned above, and also in the manuscript, *Like Love Poems*, which she eventually presented to VUP. I wanted to keep as close as possible to her original concept, using the book title and chapter headings she favoured and keeping pretty much to her ordering of the love poems in the second section. But I didn't accept all her choices. In my mind, I argued with her, I accused her of 'romanticism'. I remembered that in a letter, wittily comparing herself to her mother, Janet, she had already agreed with me! 'She, with her so fully lived life, I think would like to write a "spiritual" autobiography while I haunter of churches, naturally stay with "romance".' Yet I also wanted to celebrate her eroticism, her stubborn hopefulness, her idealistic stance: 'I / there / with my arms / open'.

Athough hardly any poems from the 'Barrys Bay' section of this book were ever presented to a publisher, Joanna had written them out by hand time and time again, as if, in ordering them, she was mediating the traumatic episodes of her life in the 1970s. As if she was distancing herself from them over the years, almost as a kind of publishing.

I first met her in 1971 when we were both teaching at St Dominic's College in Dunedin. I remember her going off in the May holidays to marry and returning unmarried. The ceremony took place later that year. I was not her confidante at this time; I knew her as a painter but not as a writer. The academic and literary worlds of the 70s were dominated by brilliant young men for whom women might well be the Other, the Lover, the Muse. But not the Poet. Attempts to express real womanly experience or the domestic were most likely to be sidelined as trivial, hysterical or hormonal.

When *Imogen* won the PEN Best First Book Award in 1978, the judge, Michael Joseph, along with Joanna, was breaking new ground. Cathie Dunsford made an interesting observation in her lengthy review of *Imogen* years later in *Broadsheet*. 'Of the three major literary magazines in this country, *Climate, Landfall* and *Islands*, only *Landfall* bothered to review the work at all. This review by Brian Turner (also entered for the award Paul won) is six lines long, sandwiched in between two longer reviews covering three pages in toto. Hardly encouraging.'

Turner himself had had this to say, 'It must have taken a lot of courage to release this work for publication; perhaps it was a necessary unburdening.' Maybe he had felt under pressure, confronted by 'the overall tone of desperation, a virtual demand that we share her grief for her dead child'. And then there was the question of what exactly was this thing that Joanna had made: 'For all one's compassion it is hard not to be left drained by the work which is more of an experience than a poem.' After all this time, look how wonderfully wrought, strong and compelling the *Imogen* poems are, even when removed from their original painterly context. Maybe this was indeed a new thing, poetry as something to be felt, something more like a painting but still made with words. Better not to limit it by conventional definitions.

'As a painter/poet I sometimes feel like a sieve or fine skin on the natural world which presses through my consciousness. A lover/receiver.' This was Joanna in her essay on Catholicism (p. 137). Several times in letters she expressed the tensions familiar to a writer, the pull between restraint and feeling, between reticence and public utterance. 'I think I'd like to keep myself in the margins,' she wrote on one occasion, then on another, 'Also one loves – needs? – occasionally to see ones own life mirrored in a poem.'

She wrote of the Banks Peninsula days herself, in her incomplete autobiography 'Rooms & Episodes I', published in *Brief* 32. There are tender family memories: 'Later Jeffrey minded Maggie mornings or Thursdays while I worked, roamed outside with my tiny super-8 camera, the Pentax, or notebook of water colours & poems.' And terrible, nightmarish moments which threatened to break her. She wrote of 'Despair creating style. Did extreme unhappiness make good poetry? I doubt it: the poems would have been better for fresh air – literary, emotional away from the valley of attrition where two conflicting cultures, values, world views were locked in stasis.' Her honesty and directness gave me the freedom to make what I would of the earliest poems in the manuscripts, and in this I have greatly appreciated the warm support of her family.

The love poems in the second section, seemingly the most private writings of this scrupulously private artist, were in fact the poems she most wanted to put out into the public arena. She adored the work of Mallarmé and Baudelaire, producing her own refreshing translations of them. Her quest for the Beloved was marked by a number of intense relationships in which heart and intellect and body all sought fulfilment. She was open to the ecstatic, punishing power of Eros, 'the violence of / love in a / quiet life', and she records the oh so human trip, as did Sappho and Catullus centuries before her, in memorable language.

In the third section of the book, 'Night & Snow', there is as it were a mighty gathering up of all that was loving and passionate, intellectual and cultivated in Joanna. Here she is vibrantly engaged with the world, alive with delight in her children, her friends and family, active in political resistance, filled up to the brim with music and beauty. Laughing and wittily argumentative. The poems date from the 1970s up to about 2000, tracking her lifeline with a depth and intensity not often found in more conventional autobiographies. But they are more than merely a record. They work away, making links between seeing and shaping, between image and word, between nature and art. Between G–D, nature and art, the driving forces of her vivid and amazingly productive life.

This work as her editor has felt to me like a continuing conversation with Joanna. Or as if I was somehow entering her dream. 'I can begin to dream / with some precision / into another series of works / with words' she wrote in an undated letter. I wrote several poems for her during her lifetime and have written more since her death. One of my favourites, from 1996, is as follows:

SHADDAI

'Could the fullness of humanity ever
have happened within the confines of The Garden?'
I'm reading to Joanna, backed into a gate
at Seacliff. Rusty padlock, rusty chain,
the land falling away. The asylum is empty.
We've eaten pickled walnut on ryebread
and brie and now she's painting the beautiful
big blue sea, her left hand
open on her thin knee. 'Did you know,
my dear, that Shaddai, the Breasted One,
is one of the many names of God in Genesis?
That the other name for Eve is Zoë, Life?
That Isaiah's prophetic poetry
was written, more than likely, by his wife?'

I sent her the poem and she wrote to me from Dunedin, on the back of a postcard of Larnach's Castle:

I love your poem but remit its ethos. I should gladly have baked bread for Isaiah. Maybe you shd buy a new house down here! Theres a v. nice one for sale across the road from me. LOVE Joanna

Yet this was the woman who wrote in her essay on Catholicism of the need to 'Rewrite the image of the Virgin Mary as scriptural earthy fertile ordinary'. And this same earthed spirituality, which I would call feminist, is there, as clear as mud in the poignant yet also nicely mischievous lines of 'On the Transfiguation'.

In conclusion, I want to quote from an essay, 'The Vanished Simple Good', that Joanna wrote for *Takahe*. She was the guest artist in issue 39, published in April 2000. This featured the eight paintings of the series 'frugal pleasures' in which she incorporated lines from Satire 1, vi by the Roman poet Horace.

> It's often a coincidence of thoughts, feelings, things on the
> table, that give rise to a painting . . . nature and culture on
> a table, sacred & profane where the table hints at ceremony
> . . . This series celebratory & valedictory.

That hits it on the head. It's what I want to say about this collection of her poetry.

Bernadette Hall
January 2006

Acknowledgements

I want to acknowledge first of all the warmth and support offered by Joanna's family: her husband, Peter Harrison; her children, Maggie, Felix and Pascal Harris; and her sisters, Charlotte, Mary and Jane Paul. Right from the beginning, getting this book out has been their desire and they have done all that they could to make the task easier.

Special thanks to Michael Nicholson for his generosity in hosting a family reading of the poems in Wellington. And to Charles Bisley for his wise advice and boundless enthusiasm. He cheerfully undertook the daunting task of getting Joanna's papers copied and set in order. Thanks to Andy Fenton of NZ Micrographics, Tawa, who digitised all the poetry manuscripts taken from Joanna's Wanganui home.

Warm thanks to Celia Thompson and also to the Quaker community in Wanganui who looked after Charles and me when we went to Joanna's house to uplift her papers.

I am grateful to Gregory O'Brien who read an early version of this manuscript and saw it as significant.

Special thanks to Brendan O'Brien who designed the book. He was one of the few people Joanna trusted to replicate the aesthetics of her work in print. And to Fergus Barrowman and VUP for their support and good coffee. Fergus was excited about the project from the start and has taken the utmost care over the finer details of production.

Thanks to Peter Ireland, Joanna's art trustee, and to Gerald Barnett of the Mahara Gallery in Waikanae. The cover painting was located through the exhibition of Joanna's drawings organised by them as part of the New Zealand Arts Festival, 2006. Thanks also to Robert Cross for the author photo.

barrys bay

Through the shaped spaces of the
beds frame; through the flower
carved in the wood & through the
window pane; through the pierced
verandah hood, the foliate rose I
see the straight & curved branches
parting of a tree.
                    Without the lens
heaven, / the heavens less understood.

miracle
as it were
a glass tree
in sunlight
after rain
the spreading
Japanese plum
transformed
to broken black
lines
& crushed diamonds
crusted with bud
& yellow leaf
is water laden
blooms not
it brilliants
in stasis
of natural art
as the
pomegranate tree
cast in iron
at Issogne
reared its black fruit
& cast down water
before the
tiered arcading
of a Renaissance
court
one of its kind
'one of its kind'

my plum tree
of ink & silver
wearing yellow blue
vermilion white
flashes
in its diadem
crowns the
blank green of the
clear lawn
framed by a
carved verandah
set against the
light & dark hill.

late summer leaves trees green til May
late autumn winds strike clothes from the line
bring rain
late morning a bird cries, rain stops
a warm clean air; & on the plushy hill
sun plays in a cobalt sky the book of hours
spun whorls of lilac mist like turret shells
& on the razor ridge white snow
lightens
I sit at my door & drink a fragrant tea
2 vessels chink in the sun a Chinese song:
& on the line a row of water diamonds

Red

is the colour of our
excited intentions;
out to dinner in a
scarlet coat, another town
some shoes among the grey
mens shoes, bottles, jeans
were scarlet
and
when our friend
took the plane
his early breakfast
as I saw it
was
brown apple piled with
cherries
a static of
excited intentions.

I had the apple, put back the cherries.

On The Beach At Waitati

the players played
volleyball tall & short
between stakes
sea to the back of them
she with blonde hair
like a lioness
punched the ball
by slightly raising her hand
the American, expert
was only playing
& patted it
toppling the net; my man
being new missed but
enjoyed the teasing
& open air,
a good day;
the child with a strange friend
clammy padded for crabs
the baby in an orange blanket
passed from woman to woman
I painted sky like butter
behind a sheer black headland
while, aft, between
dune grass & green farm
land a white ball
over & over
rose & fell &
stayed.
Those who came to the house
listened

he sideways
she face under mine, butterfly
he red mouth closed on my words
& he like a friend in mid
stream, answering,
listening
rendered me speech.

STILL LIFE

You rocked the cradle
I wrote & read
& searched an image for our childs eye
(leaf petal pool tadpole)
& said
this likening
is loving merely
& when you came to bed
the two wine glasses overlapped
the white pot plant drew close to the camellia
& one green curtain embraced the whole.

on the death of Charles Brasch

The dead we dig in dig in
His death a fishbone hard to swallow
Smiles agrees demurs
Suggests a little bread (fresh or stale?)
Keeps silence behind his mouth
Serves out love to friends
in small bone china dishes
a sweet nut clad in a thin hard shell
small helpings
How he loved!
Behind doors
Took his heart
out of an ornate box
Fought in the silence
behind his mouth
Left
gifts to be heard / poems
in the silence that ah
your words my dear
interrupt

bedside light
makes the window black
& the mirror
black
as the reservoir
today
just ruffled by the breeze
in its yellowed concrete basin
thru high wires
where a little pier led
to the wooden building
on the lake
capped with white, fretted like
a pagoda
gate feathered with ridiculous
white slats ribs of
seagulls
'just check out the reservoir
our friend jumped out of the van
turned a handle &
led thru bush to the
silent dam
showing us
how the overflow leapt & raced
down sheerest void
where
I marked
the water ran
first
thru a concrete

groove straight &
deep
narrow
(one foot wide)
flowing, quite quickly, evenly
this is your life this is your life this is your life
                              this is my life

The city sky at night is not black
PALOMA
In my window a white house
turns
its square pale brow
diffuse lights from the city
define no contours
cut out house not stuck on but
blank in the dimness
A boxed in porch
juts out an outside light
shapes & sharpens a window
to the point of recollection –
8 square panes & the clear creases of curtains:
these shadows contain my childhood
grey dark grey night white

ii.

Angel of childhood fat dove
wooden mother
you open to a dim bedroom
where light under door or a night light
sharpens an edge
of effaced furniture
angle of wardrobe patch of carpet
or the arc of homecoming carlights
discovers the pattern of walls

iii.

Toy mother empty cotton reel spare
wardrobe lost thimble
House
you live when light jumps to an
upstairs window
3 am
Someone wakes from the forest
sees the abandoned book shelves step
forward
pulls the real doll to her bosom
and turns down
white paths to childhood

The room is close with mystery
this morning
heavy green folds of velvet curtain
are patterned with light
the sky breaks in panes of almost blue
& casts a white mirage upon the
ceiling
mirror filled with things
the white dove-cote outhouse
received from another window
with its dark apertures
a mound of sunlit ivy
a light blue room
caught, held in the
round lid of some vessel
open on the dressing table.
Or so the room seems to be
heavy & punctuated with mystery
in the early stillness & I would
drift out & put on the room, the day
a close & heavy garment
for my pregnancy,
but the obdurate shape by my side
prevents my peaceful
mingling with the folded curtain & the light
the mirror the window the pale day . . .

Time drifts out & leaves a wake of sand
& my unbeing on the shore
he stands between myself & my own self

as the strong beat of his music from
an upper window
prevents my moving out into the wide
green spaces of the garden
& so I stand in the Pass of un
completeness day after day
while everyday he completes himself
in his appetites
in the continuous rhythms of his music
he pushes away the jam jar satisfied

I turn to him to hold him in my arms
the obdurate one
& broken at last in love
I hold him in my wide embrace
which rings him with the sunlit room
the garden the house & all the valley walls.

a rising white arc
& beside him
the child squats
by the stream

Make yrself an arc
encompassing ivy laurel & plum
wherein doves
th hammock the ladder th stone
apollonian dionysiac
Make yrself an ark
encompassed with pitch & brine, caulked
wherein doves
Make yrself an arch
a bow of laurel, willow
encompassing strength & woe
wherein doves
          & that plum
Make yrself an arc
a bow
encompassing flood & that blue
wherein doves

I cannot write a sonnet
that opens from rooms to measured
rooms with windows partitioned into
panes
  but
    only
       another
         poem
          called
             CAVE
          centre
         hollowed from the
      ever   earth
    no lights or limestone ornaments
  but space
hollowed by the shape
of its
    inhabitant

WIND

(sitting down to write a poem

with a glass of

ASH

return to Coromandel

'Go'

Miss 3 throws

six

dont count that

SUN

In the evening

we like to sit

(he in the sitting room with the

T.V.

((She has a record in her bedroom

in the kitchen is the radio

SAND

and read:

(((The *Character* of the pains varied very
much: most frequently they were of a hammering,
throbbing or pushing nature . . . pressing & dull . . .
boring with sense of bursting . . . pricking . . . rend
stretching . . . piercing . . . & radiating . . .
PETERS, 1853

SEA –

looking down on plates that flowed

colour

we said : we sd

he sd – he said:

do you / believe in everlasting?

life

  –

TITLE;

When
that broken sash window
in Port Chalmers
crushed
my finger
suspending me
while
thru the empty pane
people came & went
opened & slammed
car doors until
I fainted fell &
woke, I left
an orderly débâcle:
one curtain rod sloped across the frame;
the heavy curtain in thick folds on
the floor;
one carved oak footstool parallel the wall,
as formal & exact
as the cubist cuirasses
greaves, visors
among which Bresson's
Lancelot dying sits &
says his lady's name.

a white heron
standing over
a muddy estuary
twice the span
of the telegraph pole's
cross timbers
it was mounted on
sometimes its twisting
would shape up
the sinuous back-
arching of its neck
mostly it was still
simply a big
upended rectangle
a white stamp
on green bush
over the muddy
estuary
a white bird
stood me through
the long & cumbered
trek the rotting apples
& wrong arrangements
wrangles of the day
a white heron

SYCAMORE TREE

The tree
jarred & grated
in the wind

woke us
with harsh birds
at dawn

scratched &
prevented
our going

by the house
wall.
why

is the axe
under
your window?

The sycamore
is down

now

silence
at night &
by morning

mastless

the house
flaps wide
to the wind.

The axe
is laid
at the roots
of the house.

We must go.

but it is always spring

for D.

A little feverish tonight
to draw the yellow jug
of jonquils on their
green stems, to draw
their green stems &
the grey shadows cast
on the jug
against the black
fire place with the
little creaking flames

There are red glasses
on the glass table & an empty
yellow bowl

a bronze tray with a letter
on it, a page that is
blue like the sky
the shadow of the
jonquils

& under the glass
are pinioned
scarlet cherry leaves
& I remember
even in the spring
that it is always autumn

a sick girl

the peonies shatter the shade with their red bodies
their hotness splinters my eyes
til the white curtain returns its kind whiteness

(IMOGENS)

mouth
                        like
a goldfish mouth is
                                working at the breast
blue/wet & slippery
the milk
        flows
                        down
in the blue wet/mouth
                        lights shine
from the yellow shade   in the blue room
                        here / now
that loose white ear
                like an (orange) oyster
                                (smoked)
& the (lamp lit) tongue flashes out & in
                        the corner of her codfish mouth

                like

hand (not by the eye) seen
                        tongues
                                        of
shellfish (cockle) under the sand as the tide slips over
                                                at dusk

little fish
      (baby)
don't learn
      to
      walk
      on
      knives
        !

probe prove probing probable probity
                              proboscis

I probe
she you Imogen probe probes probe
        the forefinger
        the extended forefinger
                        touching

each   each thing
I at the nerve end en
countering
each change of en
                viron skin

        I   touch thing
        I   touch I in touching
        I   touch thing touching me
        touching

The finger forefinger on either hand
                    makes a direction
            hesitates   on the air
            stabs   with diffidence
            once   twice   once

& curls finger curls
round   (that & the next finger

thing

    when
    comes
    thru the air   slowly
    diffidently   certainly
    the other (either fore
                finger to
    touch curl round   ex

    change.

  Where were we, Descartes?

      p r e c i s e

        Let us start with the finger

for Bill & Marion

The flowers swell & swell at me
across the hospital room
across
greased lino
swell
yellow & blue;
next
a brown paper rubbish
bag
a white striped
towel a
stainless steel
sink in
fluorescent light
fluoresce
yellow chrysanthemums
yellow carnations
the yellow lobes of
irises
that are altogether
blue
& keep saying it:
their silence is inexhaustible –
this kind of conversation
I have never quite had with you, my friends
before
(the leaves are very cool and dark & smell good)
        yellow, yellow
          & blue.

thursday – thursday

delivered of a baby &

again
      delivered of
               a baby
from the womb of living
to the life of night

9 months from her birth to her weaning
          gate to her berth
9 months of imperfect breathing
I her mother labouring her death
        heavy breasted cementing
        her cradle in the earth
        made her path straight

another pairing: mother with a lily
framed in the doorway; dear friend with a
        cyanotic rose

the blonde sweet nurse assisting at the birth
the doctor who cut the cord

cordis   ;   corda

afterward : the hallowed days
        scoured by God.

Room before the womb
catacomb
green blue green
of sea & grasses seen
in dream
the bed a night-blue
pall
the windows
veiled the glass
opaque
the carpets pattern
flowers beneath the sea
3 white vases stand
against the wall
empty
unless one
cup a
drained camellia
the black
wooden idols
horns decrescent
grown
Corots woman
flesh of stone
her black gown
black McCahon
the door shut
on now
a white shawl

My soul has
dreamed its
images of
absence
my sleeping child
white face
closing round the
black mouth
white fingers curling
on a dark palm
the child
sleeping on a
rim of
white breast
a white house re
ceding in the
half night
white mantle
rising on a
green wall
no fire no grate no
anathemata but
one white clock
closing round an
empty dial
one white vase
holding a leafing
branch
ivory china alabaster
pointed with the
spectrum
but the green leaves part
on no degree but O
white white white white white

fallen from the room
asleep or
awake

profoundly
undreaming I
changed &

returned

the walls trumpeted
the trumpet sounded
my love witch doctor angel
mage
had burst the
tomb with
orange azure scarlet
citron crimson pink

& summoned
   me
      from
         the
waiting chamber
   to
      the
green womb
whose walls are
wet with
blood

Big with it
I left your bed
& lay down
in the garden
on damp ground.
Saw through the tent's flap
black windows
vacant spaces
in the night's grey
& nearby scattered lights
of the moon
on white flowers.
That black gap
& the smaller
joined by a narrow frame
told of the child's passing
or of mine.
And a white crown.

A black mother
Lives inside me
Dreaming of death
Dreaming the Irish shipwreck
Walking the shore
Observing the black mussel bed
The blackened bodies
The toothless comb
The open handbag
A small round mirror
Paper in water
The ink running –
A black mother
Lives inside me
Dreaming of death

WEATHER

It's only the weather that makes me cry.
Endless winds worry high
branches all night & their sound is a dry
roar. Strange to hear wind strive
& no rain. If there were rain
I would not cry.

It's only the weather makes me cry
out. Mists creep from the valley
dissolve from the ridges, blocking
mouth & ear & nose & eye
breath where none is. If the moon would shine
I should not outcry.

It's only the weather makes me numb.
Winds that wrestle hassle tussle fret
while the sky stays blue & the sun is high
hot winds from the south brassy winds drum
a circus sky. If the day were quiet
I should not be dumb.

What your heart understood my heart would reply
were the weather good I should not want to die

when my child
on my knees
hits my face with
dirty hands
& grasps my nose
& presses hard
something
breaks inside me
like the
yellow greeny stalk
of a lily
when my husband
says you'll do it my way
its white head
drags in the dust

RONDO

and I'm crying
bitter as hell
& the sun streams in
thru the window
over the loud yellow jonquils
catching the scarlet tablecloth
& music pours out of the
window
embroiders the sunshine
& I'm crying I'm
bitter as hell

I am an open window
a black barn door
light pours ceaselessly
outside
the glass is broken
the pane
the barn is empty
I am a schoolhouse
stuffed with straw
a white post
a ruined landscape
I am an open
& banging door
two chimneys
(the light passing through
the pain
let night
hide / let slide / my
dismemberment

for every grief a flower!
my garden is riot of crimson
           orange & black mouthed
           tulips
a curse
           there blooms suddenly a
           pale petunia in the hot
           house green
a blow
           & there are clanging
canna trumpeting
           the middle of the garden
           heart sickness
there spreads heartsease
a smooth bank to lie down on
           is the heart heavy
here is a branch for swinging
           the heart muffled
           attend to these small & speaking
violets
           violence a prison
           a deaf dead ear
           raise by degrees
           child yr wounded
           eyes to the light
           to the sweet pasture
           & the trees hear my
           voice in the wind &
           lean yr mouth against
           the rind speak into the breeze

you are known
even as you know

                  to our delight

like love poems

Flares

less your small kisses on my neck
while dancing
than
your look of one
climbing through sea
towards a light

ii)

that one, his
white & slightly
shiny, blind &
listening face
held to mine
like a moon,

iii)

his look sweeping
like lighthouse   beam
faltered
to
blindness of
night thing unmasked
by
light

PRONOUNS

'I,' said my husband; never, 'we'
'You,' said my sister; never 'we.'
'We are up here,' he said
so when I followed him
the bands were playing; strangers
or friends round
the imaginary table;
but it was solid wood,
& laid for two.

for M.K.

His eyes

he
held onto me with
his eyes

until
trembling an idea
arose

like
a small boy on the
brink

or
him having the ball
&

I
there with my arms
open

the conversation

How beautiful the fish here piled
up all different sizes gleaming
filleted on marble slabs the
fins sluiced away
her body curving under the
light the flesh (of neck
face & hands) white his
head bent forward, in
shadow.

At your visit

(my voice too careless
& the light too bright)

a drawer, my
heart
long jammed
shut, falls

open

Lake Wiritoa 2

the water is 'beautiful,' 'beautiful'
& 'fucking lovely'
a thin woman
leans over a child with great
tenderness
the hills are yellow
a man's body
white on
grey gold
water

I saw the young white faced man at the pub
& then 3 or 4 times again in the week —
ducking into a ski shop in the afternoon
& again in town where he touched me lightly
on the shoulder
& on the bus next to me his face
full of expression the noise of the bus
completely drowning his words
he got out with me; & there he was
at the poetry reading, face strained upwards
with a white intensity listening

but
        why were you not there
        why were you not there
        why were you not there
        why were you not there

I thought
I had not thought of you
but crossing the public library
you crossed my mind
as if
taking from my old worn purse
the pocket mirror
I found my face —
still there

the dilettante

on Monday I was incurably ill
on Tuesday I talked all night
on Wednesday I slept all day
on Thursday I fell in love
on Friday I said goodbye
This was an extraordinary week
This was an ordinary week.

BLUE FLEUR

the french doors are half
open
like an embrace
the window is just open like
a promise
the thin cotton curtain falls softly
like
a caress
inside
the rooms are airy and articulate
blue mint green and terracotta
where shall I hide

autumn / winter

I am cold
I buy a red cardigan
scarlet
will warm me
I am cold
lacking your arms
around me

harried
from the house
by my daughter's anger
I feel naked
in my light shirt
I dress myself
in a green bracelet
clasping a white stone

letting go pain
I wonder at the mystery
of a young girl's growth

pushing aside
longing
I can find comfort
in your regard.

, like sheep

Friend,
I want to make a confession to you
that I left the way
and pushed up thru blackberry, straining
the delicate fence
observing without joy
the young pistachio nuts set against
rock terraces,
in the faintness
of effort anxiety for the child
and heat
when I heard a voice call out
there's gorse, go back to the stile.

I confess
that I shrank from the long
path up the tall hill with the child
the fine path, the wooden bridge
netted for ease of the feet
or the way back
thru jumpy steers
to the road.

Is all morality
metaphor?

            (and we like sheep . . .

in shaking my hand
he let it go

he took my
hand
in order to
let it go

he did not take my hand
he let it go

I did not meet his
eye
he did not keep
my hand

he shook my hand
off

he took my hand
he did not take my hand

neither of us was there.

BRISE MARINE

The flesh is sad, alas – & I've read all the books.
I must escape. Escape. I sense that birds are drunk
from staying between the strange foam & the sky.
Nothing, not even old gardens reflected in eyes
Can hold this heart that drowns itself in sea
O nights, not the vacant shine of a poor lamp
on empty paper that still guards its whiteness.
And not the young woman nursing her infant.
I will leave. Steamer steadying your mast heads
Raise anchor for an exotic nature!
Ennui, disturbed by cruel hopefulness
trusts yet in the great farewell of waved handkerchiefs.
And maybe the masts, inviting storm clouds
are among those that a wind brings to wrecks
lost without masts, without masts or fertile small islands . . .
But listen my heart to the song of the sailors!

translation of a poem by Mallarmé

Green River – for C.

2 versions

your green look
lapped my face

a green river
lit the face
that shadowed mine

you came in with
laughter & en
thusiasm   ad
monitions   not
until your
kiss good
bye did we   re
sume   our
conversation

stripped of
   beauty by
wind rain heat
   hair matted
you see me now
   in silence
your yellow eyes un
   flinching against
    mine

answering needs

to Rhondda

for a 6 week holiday
one day in Wellington
for retreat 8 hours
thirsty on the meandering
bus   for joy
your blue cardigan &
electric blue stockings
running to meet me;
& when he'd stopped
talking all those little lighted panes
& stars,
romance.

walk back
over the line of my laughter
to the shore of my friendship
(your sky blue trousers flapping, to
where I wait your golden child on my
lap
don't look at the drop
(I have my arms across my eyes)
my shoes are too new, too un
familiar to put foot after foot on the high
wire risking
death
walk across the wire (the river light
unsettled me, blame the
river, & up the
bank to your wife waiting
in her round hat
waiting even & always with
gaiety,
love.

I wanted to say
I was hurt today
when unfamiliar sounds
in the garden
became a hedgehog
erect & moving
in broad day
it stayed
I pulled away
the grasses caught
about its head
& went away
& later found it
still there/& looked
& it was under/spiked
I took a stick
& forced it off
& found a neat round
hole, & on the iron
pole, a touch of
enamel,
but your voice on the phone was
dry, dry.

TELEPHONE CALL

As you speak
to me
the room fills up
and our friends
file in
summoned one
by one
our voices
grow quiet
and faint

and admitting to being
outnumbered
we say
goodbye

I would like to throw up my arms
and dive
below the surface
of tomorrow with
its happy arrangements
morning tea with the Americans
the private view –
direct to
the day after tomorrow
and resume my life
in the empty room
not out of hearing of
the telephone
tuned to the deep intent
in the almost certain
silence of the
telephone

NOW

I lean against the wall
in my blue kitchen
waiting for the telephone
I am like a Sarasati bride
that leans against the wall
among companions
silent fasting unmoving
on view like wedding presents
for days while
downstairs the feasting
continues

poem written in a garden

the days were crowded there was no room
to write about the poetry of things
the sage green tablecloth that brought
the grass into the room
the pink rose in the honey-jar that made
the field a garden
(the rose meaning love or grace
or just a witness to the hand out a window plucking
it
you gone: and the coffee pot
still bends at the knee slightly
like Rodin unguarded in his studio
like the beloved standing as if he wishes
to be entirely
seen:
dictionaries piled up
give the room a mannish look
& those blue flowers, corn flowers
against the dark
panelling
dark as inscrutable sea walls in
shadow, as an altar by Bellini,
dark as the inside of a rabbit's
ear
declared their poetry, I said
but un
translatable to one who couldn't
see
the face of the beloved
framing them.

The Silence of Trees

When you applied the tourniquet
your voice was kind
I cannot feel the pathways to the heart
and whiteness rests my mind.

Not at the end
but in the middle
Goodbye like the kernel of the apple
the hard shaft of the spindle.

Sitting beneath the protected tree
too near to see its height
I ponder the foolishness of she
who daily placed a stethoscope
to her own heart.

Downstream
the barge is moving away
canopied in white and candle lit
how sad this is and yet
not sad, the death of love
without the loss of it.

meditation on blue

sudden spears of
Agapanthus open
blue on grey
Pohutukawa
with the violence of
love in a
quiet life

night & snow

O

Something about
being
at the centre
of a
big floury rose
tilted back
All lines
converge
at the
centre
Perspective
(Alberti's
isn't true
We've all
heard of
gravity
Earth
  O
Apple
 Eve
  I
  O
Thou

What
 who
  am
   I
talking

about
makes the
scene
composes
the picture
reads (writes)
the poem
joins the
arch
of the
sea
but
thou
  O
eye
(look look
it's in
my pictures
all lines
converge
at the centre
not the middle
but
just outside
the picture
here
  O)

I'm sick
like in
the books
but know
all lines
converge
at the
centre
  O

Blackwood
controlled
his house
by invisible
threads
said
the boy
(you O)
He died
(What happened
to the centre?

There was
one who
lost the reins
put his head
down
And one
fled within his
household
patterns
like a moth

God is
his own
housekeeper
(he died)
what happened
　　O
Etruscans
in the tomb
held
one man
(like the rest)
held
between thumb
&
forefinger

an egg
greeting
blessing
crude sign
of rising   O

Lawrence knew
& held up
his fingers
Not a thousand
but one man
survives

egg
oval
& not a
printers O
we only know
the circle
by its
absence
whiteness
perfection
ditto
ontology by
zero
the oval
earth
shaped by
forces
preponderant

I am sick
like in the books
can feel the
death
inside me
like a

baby
'by a rose thorn
blackened towards Eros'
the seed shaking
in the blousy
petals

It was not like that
but I can't
get off
the page
    O
I   O   thou
who
completes
the
arc
of the
sea
but
thou O eye

Shaking of
the seed
not to generation
turgid round
(I can't get off the page)
not in the
wind in the
earthquake
in the rushing
fire
shaking
at the
still
small
    o

an ear
to hear
a seed
to bed
& bleed
a word
to grow
hip
at the
centre
of the
rose
   O

(You hold it
like you
hold the
page
between
thumb
& forefinger
red man
couchant)

JOURNEY

in memoriam Iain Lonie

All day
I read poems
gleaning pieces of
landscape
look up
it rushes by
backwards
sheep on its back
& birds on the backs
of sheep shaven white
in the late afternoon
is it Canterbury
sun

We all get out
I don't read
we look so odd
sitting on rucksack
or standing
shorts and walking boots
or pink and shoulderless
or picnic *en famille*
in this wide grassy
stony space
beside the parked
train

Pale tawny country
turquoise sea stripe
pulled past

read it quickly
left to right
and sleep uncomfortable
sifting words and
trees
wake to recognise
the face
under the plum tree
sunburnt searching serious and
kind

Event at Kaikoura
an alsatian
jumped from the
luggage van
the little boy was full of
story the mother
cried

for Felix

a black shawl over a chair
& the corner
composed itself.
the light came from outside
& delayed/on the
delphinium
& behind the oak trees
1 2 3
a grey stripe
is a tennis court
& men have
white shirts only
& sometimes
arms
while the ball
flying/occasionally
thru trees
keeps the moon
in motion.

You necessary weight sail anchor
Bulb to ground
Bone to socket
Pestle   mortar
Stone lying on stone

My friend has a slab of black wood
Grooved with circular hollows
8 cupholes
2 each end &
6 lined up between them
quick brown hands move
conch shells lain in the hollows
when the hand finds a place that is empty
your turn ends

                space

The first dead lay under stone
                cut under with cupholes

Between the camellia & the white jug
lines of red & black
pattern of space
complexity   black
hewn   wood   space
palimpsest   cupola   cavity

                space

black   rock   lingam
camellia   space
dented and
fringed at its edges
by volute camellia
and saw toothed rosemary
cut by a
straight white milk
jug

          camellia

for Mary

making tea
she wore
a blue towel only &
knotted hair
the floor was washed
& windows
the baby smelled of
soap
& summer wind
blew through
open doors

for Maggie

OBJECTS OF VERTU,
IMAGES OF GRACE

a small silver brooch, a plain calyx
      on a poet's shirt
a little glass vessel, 'slumped' silver
      rimmed

IMAGES OF INTEGRITY

those circles of Chinese jade I did not
      show you
the circle of pine tree tufts you
      wouldn't look at
the stone circle fountain with its two
      intimate steps
      you didn't drink from

Poem for Anne H.

brown strands of
ponga
swing in the
spring wind
like my old
brown summer dress
(cotton jersey, scooped &
flounced, worn, loved to
dereliction
'get rid of it'
said my
sister.

my sisters come
with knife and drum
'change yourself'

rude winds, rough music
shake down
great brown branches
in my small town
garden

mature green
leaves extend
black spokes
amidst brown
detritus

old burnished gowns
still hang
among the green blouses

TREE revealed in my window
as if an icicle suddenly
blossomed & branched in my heart
an ordered procession of branches
complication of sinuous twigs;
naked it stands,
athletic; absolute
erect before white mauve & emerald vapours
that drift –
it is winter:
it is the earth that flowers
as if that summer load of green
concealed the plain unfolding
of the seed.
A yellow rose
in my window
has not such extravagant
restraint
so stern tense & prolix a poise
as the consummate
wood
in the season of its
speaking.

the Course

trying to feel the bottom of this poem
feel its circumference
ground on something hard.

the salt marsh
seemed to go on for ever.
2½ hours
tracking 1½ miles of
tidal mud & marsh
from the round roosting point
Otefelo Head, observing
distant heads arms feet, the
bus driver a tea wagon

PLANTAGO CARORUPUS   *traversing the grey marsh, it was*
SALICORN AUSTRALIS   *fluent with colour –*
TRIGLOCHLIN STRIATUM   *red russet yellow pink indigo*
SELLIERA REPENS   *the floating horizon iridescent*
SAMULUS REPENS   *water; those low lying naked*
SHOENUS NITENS   *succulents changing colour*
                            from zone to

zone; SALICORN AUSTRALIS neutral, but now its long
smooth thallus is pink to pinkish grey, & among the little dark
round leaves of SAMULUS REPENS, SELLIERA RADICANS
thews flash fleshy green; in ponds ancient snails are grey then
pink now russet brown; the men have stopped talking & stoop
very quickly intently picking up snails peculiar to ARAMOANA
3 mm long soft narrow brownish hidden among roots of
LOCHNOGROSTIS LYALLI & LEPTOCARPUS SIMILIS

salinity fluctuates from zone to zone, in wet & dry.
LOCHNOGROSTIS tolerates fluctuation is averse to sea
water
while WHEAT (our standard) cannot survive the presence
of salt
MIMULUS REPENS, SELLIERA RADICANS, SALICORN
AUSTRALIS show in ascending order their saline
tolerance.

WHEAT may germinate in sea water
while SELLIERA RADICANS depends on fresh
water at germination for low salt levels in
which to rear young plants

SALT MARSH PLANTS are confined to salt marshes
but planted elsewhere, say in a well composted
garden thrive & grow taller. They don't like
the salt marsh but they can stand it.

as I was walking tired thru cold rain to warmth
across the salt marsh beside but not exactly with
2 talking old professors – a young chap in a
round yellow hat was sitting on his rucksack
watching me

we stopped abreast
13 wooden stakes
hemming in
the sea
&
between the invisible coastline & the invisible horizon,
a symmetrical & pointed island
floating
between the 6th & 7th stake
Sunion. 'Hellas'
I said. We were standing just above the outlet
of Dunedin City Sewerage.

I only know Greece (the islands) from poems
he said.

the bus rounded
a great round water tower, concrete
at Rotary Park
high over the peninsula
& down, past norman ' ' lime kilns
over lava flow on limestone

to Allans Beach.

We all talked, walking also or wading
thru sand like salt
to a rocky outcrop, with pools
where the upper margin of the rocky shore
extended vertically, above our heads
marked out by periwinkles

In a rubbery pouch of brilliant transparency
someone found a glassy shrimp, only its eyes
defined

what   is the purpose of transparency
no purpose unless camouflage
most of the plankton are clear
but those at the surface of the ocean
prussian blue

unknowing

I reached a blue rock pool
round & deep
clear & still
empty & alive.

the whole grain

if I think of an aluminium smelter
at Wycliffe Bay
it is as if I had swallowed a few
saucepans
the hotwater bottle was grafted to my back
the bathtub got out with me
like a hood
as if surgeon's fingers
slipped the U.S. annual defence budget
cast in plastic
deftly between my liver &
my spleen.

the pointed breast
of PUKEMATA rises gently
over swelling shoulders &
smooth belly; the peninsula is like green bodies constantly
in gentle motion; from this
ridge above the town TE AU, Mt Charles
appears like a collarbone or rib
but in the quiet hinterland
his majestic pile confronts
her femaleness across eternal
separateness in space & time.

The small houses at Broad Bay
with iron roofs rusty or trim
are innocent as paua shells
or teeth
they will decay

only the road girds the flexible
shoreline like a brace.

Consider Dunedin.
There are no trees in the Exchange
There is no water in Water St
or sound of water
the river trapped under the asphalt
never had a name.
Walking round a web of streets
beyond the railway station
looking for the paper merchants
after 3 days fast
there was something wrong
gone haywire like a
bad dream.
This is where water was; the tidal zone
cast in a bitumen fantasy
cast off from nature

the earth is a creature
we are earth creatures

gold in veins is toxic

& by bitumen &
uranium
lead & plastic
aluminium

we are not fed

Drawing the Negative Space

I did not go to the Roman villa
It was five o'clock, & closed.
The custodian gave me
a glass of water.
I saw the bluebells
in a pool of blue
under trees
I inspected carefully &
with distaste brickwork
that was not Roman
but British Railway
I did not go
to the Roman Museum
at Bath
but sitting outside, sipping
medicinal waters
from a glass, our eyes dwelt on
angels, climbing ladders
up the abbey wall
angels no-one had interfered with
in eight centuries.
I did not meet Richard
Davenport, but saw him from above
like a villager in a Stanley Spencer
painting, hover in the garden
talking, gentle in the Cotswalds
light. I picked white hyacinths
& white daffodils
from a Cotswald orchard.
I did not draw them.

I did not go to Hampstead.
Did not see the artist, the private view
I did not go to Charleston
I did not go to Kettles yard
Did not enter the Queens House at Greenwich
Or the noble Banqueting House by Jones
I saw the outside only.
I never found the Physic Garden
I looked for the Physic Garden
But stepped over a small cord at Kew
to walk up a pleached walk
walking with my sister.
I did not go to Lyme Regis
I did not take the bus
that went there & back in a day
I did not go to Lyme Regis.

House Rules

A. wont have the silver spoons
in the washing machine
& B. doesn't like the blue handled set
put back in the drawer
In their house I misplace
the lemon squeezer
Where are the big knives?
My mother takes out
my granny bonnets
from the square glass vase
& replaces them with roses

Religion is not much to do with faith, I think
& everything to do with housekeeping

St Francis de Sales
told Madame de Chantal
your heart should be as flexible
as your glove
Flexible
as the heart of Mme de Chantal
as her small hand drooping
yet submissive
in her lap
the large white hands of the rector
spread out in the illumination
of faith
white blunt and flexible
as fish.
Thought allied to feeling
sometimes moved the whole body
of the Jesuit forward
articulate with the love of
St Francis de Sales
supple with the spiritual exercise
of St Ignatius Loyola.

On board the ferry
the grey frocked French nun
when not laughing
was looking at the sea.
Her features & her speech
were incisive.
She was less interested in
my questions than in
my children.
    '... & *her* name?'
'Magdalena.'
Like the foundress of my order
Madeleine.
Our founder was a North African monk
who lived in solitude last
century.'
    '... or do you teach?'
'Our aim is to be
in the presence of the people.'
On the Kaikoura coast
she bought a filled roll
& walking the length of
the railway station
leaned against a car bonnet
& bit
into the horizon.

On the Transfiguration

the Jesuit said

how would you paint the resurrection?
'I see it as detail only in black & white.
a photograph, feet in mud, his ankles swelling
against the distant flare of dawn, dark
earth spreading to a low horizon'

& replied

'your resurrection portrays
sharing in life to me but what of
receiving life . . . not an old life but a
new life?'

the door swings
onto the smell of wet concrete
warm chlorine
    high up
I see a white dress hanging
thru the mesh
    & beside me
a girl bends tying on a white
figured skirt over
slender beige legs & panties
joined at the hip
    at the pool
a woman stands waiting

blonde hair knotted, crimson
jacket merging with the clothes
of the baby she is holding
framed by grey plate glass
    that opens on
a brilliant lawn white legs
& stems of silver
birch trees.
Her skirt is white.
    again that night
'you look beautiful in blue'
'I only notice women wearing
white, like you.'
let us put up 3 tents to celebrate
the change over.
    now
we are in a bright office
3 women talking about the transformations
in our lives
when our laughter & the light
strikes
a chain of women hurrying past the window
heads bent their eyes flash disapproval;
they are angry crying praying
O *let us join them.*

PROPER NAMES

when
the wave came
across the TOMBOLO
we laughed ANNA
pursued the floating kit
thermos lid & I
rescued the BUCKINGFORD
English mould-made paper
sodden but colours re
freshed the sky THALO BLUE &
THALO CRIMSON (the sea) the
empty beach, somewhat
vermilion
another wave came
200 yards &
recessed
        leaving
the beach empty
of horses, my shoes,
SUZETTE with little
pierced black straps
ruined
then
we took a bus
to ST PATRICKS
had a milkshake at
the NEW ADELPHI MILKBAR
somewhat confused
ANNA apologised
&
left
ANNA ANNA ANNA ANNA

AFTERMATH

waves
surge in like music
retreat with a sigh
leaving
capuccino lace
(cream on umber)
while a wash
of cerulean
lights a copper sea

waves
patterned like
the shadows of lavender
floating
lilac green in
the cup of a nervous
morning infusion

like the green on green
(sage on viridian)
saucer's arabesque

waves
like a conversation
that moves from bliss to bliss
invoking
green & green
(jade & olive)
in Katherine Mansfield's story

& the white pear trees
nocturnal flowering
(cream on umber)

in an affinity
of subtle regret, unspoken irony
& tempered pleasure.

Music at Marama

i.
the pianist lifts her tall neck
her towering neck, playing Schubert
& summer throws red carpet red
into the face of the blonde girl
fingering the music.

ii.
these girls have not conferred about
their dress the pianist in blonde
flouncy blouse green satin skirt
& new white pumps is evening
dressed for Brahms,
Janet in purples clashing sings
new music
only the girl beside the pianist
is dressed naturally, & looks out
of place.

iii.
the soprano stands against the
piano like a T-square face fierce,
hands knotted, striped skirt
become piano, necktie the india
red of mezzanine or window
russet, her pleated collar caught
into the worry of her face;
voice very loud – only her
breasts are left not knowing

what to do & rise & fall
in their own rhythm, pinkly
shadowed, gently lit.

iv.
this girl's face is brown shadowed
impassive as a jug; it is under
her hands over her shoulder
that the song takes place

v.
when someone in the audience
puts up a hand to screen the
winter sun, that big plump
white illuminated hand melts
into the white flesh of forehead
to be framed by shiny tangled
brown hair, & plushy blue
creased cloth on well filled frame

that moment is pure English
Renaissance while on stage
flutes bubble fin de siècle Paris.

vi.
the piano goes continuo
the violin up & down in the
Baroque manner; why is face
important bow slithering from
note to note she hangs her
hair like a brown curtain;
beauty she should know is
insignificant beside the
human requisite of eye
nose mouth.

vii.
there is tarpaulin over the balcony
the piano is draped
Chris at the switchboard
'this music should be rich, exciting,
also rich' proffers only hair
today I shut my eyes & ears
& hear
Lilburn's childhood clocks.

NATURE & ART

for Pascal

Pukeko country
says the boy
Monet country
I murmur
as we come to the
arched bridge, the water lilies
the old pergola that has wisteria in season
on a dry hiatus
bridge to pergola
is planted rosa rugosa
a deep vermilion tudor rose
a euphuistic
conceit, in
pukeko, Monet
country.

Notes

I have tried to leave a clear track of where the original copies of the poems may be found. In most cases there were multiple drafts, most of them handwritten. Every now and then there was a typed-up version, finality sanctioned as it were by technology. And then there were the beautiful handmade books. I found that I could not always rely on the format used in anthologies. I have indicated where and why I deviated from these published versions, and I have also confessed to the one and only violence I offered to one, and only one, text [p. 74]. That was one argument I couldn't bear to let Joanna win.

The epigraph is a two-line text within the painting 'in memoriam Christopher Canter 1954–1999 spring'.

One: Barrys Bay

Joanna had gathered together one group of 23 pages under the title 'Barrys Bay'. On the second page of this sequence there is the heading 'Poems September 1974'. There is a second grouping entitled 'Barrys Bay II', which consists of 36 pages. The date on the second page of this grouping is 'Summer 74–75'.

[17]   'Barrys Bay', p.3. Note on page: 'July'. Also in 'Songs of Seven Seasons'.
[18]   'Barrys Bay II', p.23. Also in 'Songs of Seven Seasons'.
[20]   'Barrys Bay II', p.13. Note on page: 'winter'.
[21]   'Aligning' (79-82). Published in *Morepork* 1, 1979.
[22]   'Aligning' (79-82). Published in *Morepork* 1, 1979.

[24] 'poems: Seacliff June 1973, poems for Mary'. Also in 'Infant / unspeaking', section: 'Pupureal, poems for Ingrid Magdelena b. 1973'; and in 'night & snow, poems 1972/1973, for Mary', section: 'WINDOWS / NO WINDOWS'.

[25] 'poems: Seacliff June 1973, poems for Mary', heading: '3 poems on a death'. This is the third poem in the group.

[26] 'poems 82'.

[28] 'poems: Seacliff June 1973, poems for Mary'. Also in 'night & snow, poems 1972/1973, poems for Mary', section: 'WINDOWS / NO WINDOWS'.

[30] From a handwritten manuscript with the heading 'copied from indecipherable poem in notebook c. 1975'. A note in the margin says 'copy 1999'. An alternative version, also handwritten, is towards the end of 'Barrys Bay II', no page number. The most significant difference is in the last stanza: 'I turn to him & hold him in my arms / complete at last in love / hold him in my wide embrace / that rings us with the sunlit room / the house the garden / & all the valley walls.'

[32] 'Barrys Bay II', p.17. Also in 'Songs of Seven Seasons'.

[33] 'Barrys Bay', p.16. 'August'.

[34] 'poems: Seacliff June 1973, poems for Mary'.

[35] Handwritten in 'poems & writings 76/77', on the inside page 'Dunedin'. Published in *Morepork* 3 and *The Penguin Book of Contemporary New Zealand Poetry* (edited by Miriama Evans, Harvey McQueen and Ian Wedde, 1989).

[38] Published in *Morepork* 1. Note on handwritten version: 'Dunedin 79 (?)'.

[39] 'Barrys Bay II', first poem, no page number.

[40] 'poems: Seacliff June 1973, poems for Mary'.

[42] 'poems 1999 also some early poems recovered circa 1975'. Handwritten note on back of page: '1 musket = 2 tattooed heads / = 2 tons of potatoes / = shipload of flax'.

[43] 'Barrys Bay II', p.34. Also in 'Songs of Seven Seasons'.

[44] *Imogen* (Hawk Press, 1978). Winner of the PEN Best First Book of Poetry Award, 1978. Manuscript cover: 'Imogen an elegy'; front page dedication: 'to IMOGEN ROSE February 28–December 9 1976 farewell brave heart arohanui'. Also published in *The New Poets: Initiatives in New Zealand*

Poetry (edited by Murray Edmond and Mary Paul, Allen & Unwin, 1987); and *An Anthology of New Zealand Poetry in English* (edited by Jenny Bornholdt, Gregory O'Brien and Mark Williams, Oxford, 1997).

[46]   *Imogen* (Hawk Press, 1978). Also published in *Yellow Pencils* (edited by Lydia Wevers, Oxford, 1988).

[48]   *Imogen* (Hawk Press, 1978). Also published in *Yellow Pencils* (edited by Lydia Wevers, Oxford, 1988); and *An Anthology of New Zealand Poetry in English* (edited by Jenny Bornholdt, Gregory O'Brien and Mark Williams, Oxford, 1997).

[49]   *Imogen* (Hawk Press, 1978). Also published in *Yellow Pencils* (edited by Lydia Wevers, Oxford, 1988).

[50]   'poems: Seacliff June 1973, poems for Mary'.

[53]   'poems: Seacliff June 1973, poems for Mary'.

[54]   'poems: Seacliff June 1973, poems for Mary'. Also in 'night & snow, poems 1972/1973, poems for Mary', section: 'Funereal'.

[55]   'poems: Seacliff June 1973, poems for Mary'.

[56]   'Barrys Bay II', p.24.

[57]   'Barrys Bay II', p.16. Also in 'Songs for Seven Seasons'.

[58]   This version with handwritten heading note: 'poems never before copied out (1974?) 1999.' Also in 'Barrys Bay II', p.29.

[59]   'Barrys Bay', p.11.

Two: Like Love Poems

Joanna wrote in a bio note in *Landfall* 193 (1997) of 'a book still in preparation called *Like Love Poems*, poems written from time to time over a period of 15 years'. She eventually submitted a manuscript with this title to VUP. The text consisted of poems and paintings organised in three section: 'Access to Lilac'; 'Green River'; 'Meditations on Blue'; (1980–1995). In a letter to her dated 15 November 2001, Fergus Barrowman explained that a decision was still to be made on this manuscript. Where I have used poems from the submitted manuscript, I have kept in mind her original ordering. However, I have also added extra poems.

[63]   *Landfall* 193 (1997). Also in ms 'Like Love Poems', section: 'access to lilac'; handwritten in a book, 'poems & writings, 76/77', note on inside page: 'Dunedin'; and one copy dated 'c. 81'; 'neck' replaced by 'cheek' only in the *Landfall* version.

[64]   *Landfall* 193 (1997). Also in ms 'Like Love Poems', section: 'access to lilac'; variant dates on different copies of the same text, 'c.81' and 'c.83'.

[65]   In ms 'Like Love Poems', section: 'access to lilac'; variant dates on different copies of the same text, 'summer 85' and 'summer 86'.

[66]   'prose poems', some of which are dated '1985/1986' and '1985 Wellington'.

[67]   *Landfall* 193 (1997). Also in ms 'Like Love Poems', section: 'access to lilac', date on manuscript 'c.1991'.

[68]   Handwritten; a poem before this in ms and written on similar paper is dated 'c.1991'.

[69]   In ms 'Like Love Poems', section: 'access to lilac'; dated 'c.83' in contents list of collection 'The Embrace'.

[70]   In ms 'Like Love Poems', section: 'access to lilac'; dated '81/82?' on one copy, '82/83' and '83' on another.

[71]   'poems 82'. Handwritten note added to a typescript: 'you who love / tell me / voi che sapete'.

[72]   'by CRUCIFIED love', note on page 3: 'Jerusalem '87'; also in typed-up sequence 'Blue Fleur'.

[73]   'by CRUCIFIED love', note on page 3: 'Jerusalem '87'; also in typescript sequence 'Blue Fleur'.

[74]   'by CRUCIFIED love', note on page 3: 'Jerusalem '87'. The version printed here is abridged. The following four stanzas have been edited out: 'you / in the singleness of your life / a mirror for the / 'selfsame' // the road promises/security but also / mystery. // forgive, Lord / my shortcuts // I will walk, over again, the walkway of / Aramoana. / Your path, where?'

[75]   'by CRUCIFIED love', note on page 3: 'Jerusalem '87'.

[76]   *cinq 5 poêmes / Mallarmé*; handwritten French with typed English translations.

[77]   'poems from the Ahu Ahu etc'. Also in ms 'Like Love

Poems', section: 'green river'.

[78] 'poems from the Ahu Ahu etc'. Also in ms 'Like Love Poems', section: 'green river'. Published in *Takahe*.

[79] 'poems from the Ahu Ahu etc'.

[80] 'poems from the Ahu Ahu etc'. Also in ms 'Like Love Poems', section: 'green river'. Typescript note on back: Joanna Paul, 9 Stark St., Drurie Hill, Wanganui.

[81] 'poems from the Ahu Ahu etc'. Also in ms 'Like Love Poems', section: 'green river'.

[82] 'poems from the Ahu Ahu etc'. One copy dated 'Dunedin 1981'. Also in ms 'Like Love Poems', section: 'access to lilac'.

[83] 'your name', a little book of poems and photos. Also in a selection, 'The Telephone', added to ms 'Like Love Poems'.

[84] 'your name', a little book of poems and photos. Also in a selection, 'The Telephone', added to ms 'Like Love Poems'.

[85] 'your name', a little book of poems and photos. Also in a selection, 'The Telephone', added to ms 'Like Love Poems'.

[86] In this form, *Landfall* 193 (1997). Also in ms 'Like Love Poems', section: 'Meditation on Blue'. A version exists in 'your name' with the poem title given as 'Blue Flowers', alongside a photograph on which is noted: 'poem written in a garden' and the date '18/xii/94'.

[87] 'The Silence of Trees'. Also in 'your name', with the stanzas in the reverse order, note on the back inside page: 'MALADY • MELODY • THRENODY'.

[88] 'Like Love Poems', section: 'Meditation on Blue'.

Three: Night & Snow

I chose this title for this section because of the very significant long poem 'O', which was originally set in a sequence of that name.

[91] 'poems: Seacliff June 1973, poems for Mary'. Also in 'poems: Wellington January 1974'; and 'poems 1972/1973 night & snow', dedication 'poems for Mary'.

[97] 'poems '83/84'. Listed with date 1984 in a contents page

among 'poems to send Ian'. Also in a booklet, 'Blue Mourning – Journey and other poems in memoriam Iain Lonie'.

[99] 'Infant / unspeaking', section: 'Bonding. Poems for Felix Sylvester b. 1978', which included photos. Note added to a typescript: 'from Felix 1979'.

[100] 'poems: Wellington January 1974'. Also in 'night & snow, poems 1972/1973', section: 'The Spaces Between Things'.

[102] This version handwritten with date 'c.78'. Also in 'Blue Fleur', within a section: 'MY HEART A HOME INHABITED BY FRIENDS'.

[103] 'Tender, poems from a croning', handwritten with inscription 'I / THOU / MAGGIE'. Also a typed version within a sequence headed ' FEAR / the / LATTICE / LOVE / the /DOOR', and an added note: *'You were aloof that day & I lacked appropriate words, trod fallen leaves; write you[r] own poem or paint it: you are one'.*

[104] Handwritten in an untitled and undated 1B4 exercise book.

[106] 'Barrys Bay II', p.32.

[107] *Parallax*, vol. 1, no. 2. Also in *The New Poets: Initiatives in New Zealand Poetry* (edited by Murray Edmond and Mary Paul, Allen & Unwin, 1987); and *The Penguin Book of Contemporary New Zealand Poetry* (edited by Miriama Evans, Harvey McQueen and Ian Wedde, 1989); handwritten copy with title page: '"The Ecology of Aramoana" 1975 University'.

[110] Typescript with handwritten note on reverse: 'Aramoana, Saturday 81/82 (?)'.

[112] Handwritten, dated 'June 98'.

[114] 'Right Relation Series'.

[115] This version handwritten and dated 'Dunedin 1983', listed in ms contents page: 'poems to send Ian'. A slightly different version, with a space where the word 'articulate' was omitted, and 'communication' instead of 'illumination', was published in 'On Not Being a Catholic Writer', in *The Source of the Song, New Zealand Writers on Catholicism* (edited by Mark Williams, Victoria University Press, 1995).

[116] 'On Not Being a Catholic Writer', in *The Source of the Song, New Zealand Writers on Catholicism* (edited by Mark Williams, Victoria University Press, 1995). Manuscript note: 'days & nights at Ahurangi'.

[117] 'poems 82/83'. Published in 'On Not Being a Catholic Writer', in *The Source of the Song, New Zealand Writers on Catholicism* (edited by Mark Williams, Victoria University Press, 1995).

[119] 'Aligning (72–82)', a sequence in which most poems are set, like this one, in Dunedin.

[120] 'poems 1999 also some early poems recovered circa. 1975', handwritten in a hard-covered book.

[122] *The Penguin Book of Contemporary New Zealand Poetry* (edited by Miriama Evans, Harvey McQueen and Ian Wedde, 1989); also listed in contents page: 'poems to send Ian', dated 1983.

[125] 'Boy Beside the Lake, poems for Pascal', which includes photos and drawings of Pascal Harris. The word BLACKWOOD is printed on the back cover of this little booklet, suggesting a publishing house name. Also in 'The Awakening', dated 'January 9-12 1998', made up of hand-printed poems and photographs.

Chronology

1945 Joanna Margaret Paul is born on 14 December in Hamilton, the eldest daughter of Blackwood and Janet Paul.

1965 Blackwood Paul dies.

1968 Graduates from Auckland University with a Bachelor of Arts degree.

1969 Graduates from the Elam School of Art, Auckland University, with a Diploma of Fine Arts.

1970 Moves to Port Chalmers to paint and write.

1971 Marries fellow artist Jeffrey Harris. They live together at Seacliff.

1972 The first solo exhibition of Joanna's paintings is held at the CSA Gallery in Christchurch.

1973 Joanna and Jeffrey move to Wellington, where their first child Ingrid Magdalena is born.

1973 Death of Charles Brasch, poet and publisher, born 1909.

1974 The family move to Banks Peninsula. The sequences 'Barrys Bay' and 'Barrys Bay II' are written at this time.

1976 A second child, Imogen Rose, is born in February. She dies in December following surgery to correct a major heart defect.

1977 Jeffrey Harris receives the Frances Hodgkins Fellowship and the family move back to Dunedin.

1977 *unwrapping the body*, later a book of photographs and poetry, is first realised as an installation in the CSA Gallery in Christchurch.

1978 Felix Sylvester is born. Joanna's book of poems, *Imogen*, is published by Hawk Press and wins the PEN Best First Book award.

1980 Publication of *Aramoana – Poetry & Polemic from Aiteuru*, to coincide with the exhibition 'Aramoana' at the invitation of the Wellington City Art Gallery. Joanna's contribution is obliquely recorded as 'concept, other pages' in the index.

1981 Writes 'poems from the Ahu Ahu', dated 'Dunedin 1981'.

1982 A second son, Pascal, is born.

1983 Joanna receives the Frances Hodgkins Fellowship at Otago University.

1984 Joanna leaves Jeffrey and, with her children, moves to Wellington. She later moves to Wanganui, where, apart from periods of working and living elsewhere, she is based for the rest of her life.

1987 Four poems published in *The New Poets: Initiatives in New Zealand Poetry* (edited by Murray Edmond and Mary Paul, Allen & Unwin, 1987).

1988 Death of the Dunedin poet, Iain Lonie, born in 1932.

1988 Poems published in *Yellow Pencils* (edited by Lydia Wevers, Oxford, 1988).

1989 Three poems published in *The Penguin Book of Contemporary New Zealand Poetry* (edited by Miriama Evans, Harvey McQueen and Ian Wedde, 1989).

1993 Joanna receives the Rita Angus Residency Award and spends the year in Wellington.

1995 The essay 'On Not Being a Catholic Writer' is included in *The Source of the Song, New Zealand Writers on Catholicism* (edited by Mark Williams, Victoria University Press, 1995).

1996 Joanna spends the year in Dunedin with her son Pascal. She is engaged in painting, writing and studying Greek at Otago University.

1997 Five poems from *Imogen* published in *An Anthology of New Zealand Poetry in English* (edited by Jenny Bornholdt, Gregory O'Brien and Mark Williams, Oxford, 1997).

1997 Poems published in *Landfall* 193.

2000 Publication of *rose*, handprinted by Brendan O'Brien at the Rita Angus cottage, Wellington.

2001 Publication of the book *the cherry now*, handprinted by Brendan O'Brien at the Fernbank Studio, Wellington.

2003 Joanna marries the Palmerston North architect, Peter Harrison, on February 25. She dies in a tragic accident at Rotorua on May 29, at the age of 57.

Selected Publications

access to lilac
Hand-printed at the University of Otago by Brendan O'Brien, 2005.

Aramoana: Poetry & Polemic from Araiteuru
Works by writers and artists, published to coincide with the exhibition 'Aramoana' at the invitation of the Wellington City Art Gallery. Printed by Wellington Public Libraries, 1980. 'Concept, other pages' by Joanna Paul.

the cherry now
Hand-printed at the Fernbank Studio, in the Rita Angus Cottage, Wellington, by Brendan O'Brien, April and May 2001. Poetry text and 4 images. 24 pages plus cover. 55 copies.

cinq 5 poêmes, Mallarmé
12 pages text, drawing on front and back covers. French texts handwritten, English translations typed.

forbidden apple – 7 poems on an unusual subject
Author's note: 'I consider genetic engineering to be the greatest departure for mankind since Adam left the Garden.' The back cover of this ring-bound book has the word 'BLACKWOOD' as a publishing house name.

Imogen
Hand-printed by Alan Loney at the Hawk Press, Eastbourne, 1978.

rose
> Hand-printed in the Rita Angus Cottage, Wellington, by Brendan O'Brien, 2000. 20 pages plus cover. Text only. 55 copies.

The Silence of the Trees
> Stitched 12-page photocopied booklet. Poem and photographs. Three copies.

unwrapping the body
> Photographs and poetry text. 32 pages plus cover. Made by Joanna Paul. The work was first realised as an installation in the CSA Gallery, Christchurch, 1977.

Handmade Books
removed from 3 Maxwell Avenue, Wanganui, by literary trustees

The Awakening
> 15cm x 16cm, 56 pages, black ink handwritten text on thick white paper, reverse blank. 17 photographs. Hard cover, navy with peach, pale blue & olive oil-slick pattern. Dated January 9–12 1998.

Songs of Seven Seasons
> 15cm x 22cm, 67 pages of black ink handwritten text and 40 pages of watercolour paintings, most pages blank on reverse; 17 pages both sides blank, at the back of the book. Hard cover.

your name
> 30cm x 44cm. 168 pages, 26 of art works, mostly photographs but also a card and drawings. Hard cover, shell pattern purple/olive on white.

Index of Titles

Index of First Lines